As an Occupational Thera
inspiration for The Meltdo
with families of children w
their behaviours when the
This means that meltdown
being naughty but a result of feeling overwhelmed either physically, emotionally or from a sensory perspective.

Children typically go into any or all of the following survival behaviours due to fear:
Fight: exploding like a volcano, which can be verbal or physical aggression.
Flight: running away and/or hiding.
Freeze: avoiding something that is overwhelming by passively ignoring or becoming defiant and digging their heels in.
Dissociation: disconnect, detached, daydreaming
Shutdown: loss of tone, sleepy, collapse

It is important to try to understand the reason for the meltdown and help parents to support their children with sensory and nurture strategies.

I hope these little books will help you.

Linda Plowden - OT, Therapy Space Bristol Ltd

Wednesday was Ben's least favourite day of the week because he always had PE and he dreaded it.

The PE teacher said, “Ben, I want you to play in goal today. So, hurry up and get changed.”
“But Sir…” protested Ben.
“What is it?”
“I’m not very good in goal.”
“So, practise will make you better!”
“Yes, ok then, Sir,” said Ben, sadly. But he knew that this was the last thing he wanted!

Ben had always wished he could play on the school team, but he knew that he wasn't any good. As he took his place between the posts he began to feel shaky with nerves. He found it really hard to catch the ball and he hated it when people barged into him when he wasn't expecting it. His balance wasn't very good and he often fell over.

He heard the other boys say, "Oh no! Ben's playing in goal? We're bound to lose now!"

Ben felt his heart sink. One mistake might let the whole team down.

The whistle blew to start the game and, for ages, the ball was up at the other end of the pitch.

Ben's mind started to wander and he went into a daydream. He sat down and began and to pick at blades of grass. He often found it hard to concentrate and was distracted by little things around him.

He noticed his laces were undone again! Oh no! This happened all the time. He could never tie them tightly enough!

Then suddenly, a voice shouted:
"Ben! What are you doing?"

Ben looked up to see the other team bearing down fast on his goal. He scrambled to his feet.

A shot came in. It wasn't a good shot. It was soft and feeble. Ben thought to himself, "I'll catch this one easily!" But somehow he missed it completely, and when he heard the other team cheering he knew that he had let in a goal. "I'm such an idiot!" he thought.

The rest of the team were angry with Ben. “How could you let in such a weak shot, you idiot?”

When the second half began, Ben was a bag of nerves. What would they all say if he made another mistake?

Soon his team scored a goal. If only the final whistle would blow! At least it would be a draw.

Then, in a flash, a high ball came flying in. Ben watched it as it sailed through the air. He jumped to save it but instead of catching it, he knocked it over the line by mistake. "Oh no! An own goal!"

Afterwards, in the changing room, the other boys called him names. "Useless!" "Cry baby!" "Loser!" Ben started to cry.

That evening at home he was very quiet.

"What's wrong?" asked his mum.

He took a deep breath and told her about his mistakes, how he had got upset and how all the children had been mean to him.

"I don't want to go back to school." he cried.

The next day, Ben's mum rang the school to ask for their help. They put her in contact with a woman called Lucy, an Occupational Therapist.

When Lucy met Ben she found out what was difficult for him and gave him some exercises to work on. "These will help with your ball skills and your balance."

He started by throwing a little bean bag from one hand to another. He learnt to watch it carefully as it went from hand to hand.
"Well done!" said Lucy.

Soon he was throwing a tennis ball against the garden wall. First he let it bounce once before he caught it with both hands together.

Sometimes he missed it, but the more he practised, the better he became.

This was fun! Lucy was right! Ben started feeling more confident and happier. He knew that practising for ten minutes every day was starting to make a difference.

Then he practised catching the ball ten times in a row with his right hand, and then with his left. When he felt ready, he practised catching it without letting it bounce at all. Soon he was throwing the ball against the wall, spinning in a full circle and still catching it most of the time!

At school during break, Ben watched the other children playing football and wished he could join in.

He eventually plucked up the courage to ask, “Can I play?”
“You?” they said, meanly. “Why would we want you on our team?”
“You’ll only lose us the game.”.

But then one kind boy said, “Come on, let him play. It’s only a kickabout.”

So Ben stood in goal and hoped he wouldn't make a bad mistake when a high ball flew into the box. He was surrounded by other boys, some jostling him.

He concentrated on watching the ball and, determined to get to it, he reached his arms out high above him, jumped as high as he could and caught it with both hands.

Someone said, "Good save!", and he felt a warm glow inside him.

The next time the football team played, Ben was picked to play in goal again. None of the other boys complained this time.

Ben knew that he might make mistakes again, but everybody does sometimes.

Soon, once he had made his first save, he felt his confidence grow and that warm feeling come back again. He felt 'just right'.

Postscript

Ben has a diagnosis of Developmental Coordination Disorder (DCD), sometimes known as Dyspraxia (or being clumsy). This means he finds gross motor and fine motor coordination skills very difficult. He is distractible and he feels he is bad at sports and other children make fun of him at school. He is always on the outside of games and gets picked last in PE for team sports.

His meltdown is going into a dissociative state by daydreaming making it almost impossible for him to function effectively.

An Occupational Therapist will support a child like Ben by teaching a skills program at home and school to build up his confidence with both gross and fine motor challenges. Catching is a particular problem for Ben, so grading a program by first starting with a balloon and moving to a tennis ball will help him succeed in developing hand eye coordination skills.